EXTRAORDINARY
Old Testament people

3V
Bible Studies

06 07 08 09 10 11 12 13 14 15—10 9 8 7 6 5 4 3 2 1

MANUFACTURED IN THE UNITED STATES OF AMERICA

Cover Design by Keely Moore

Contents

This Bible study focuses on three key tools for exciting Bible study: comprehension, interpretation, and application.

About

3V Bible Studies

What's the Text? begins by simply reading the Scripture passage for what it says. Then it invites deeper understanding by having us examine and ask questions about the text.

What's the Context? looks at both the literary issues and the cultural and social situation. The information in this section may address specific terms used in the passage, the character of the particular book of the Bible, what comes before the passage, what comes after it, and the events and cultural expectations of the times. Having this "story behind the story" provides important information for understanding the text and its meaning.

What's Next?, the third section, recognizes that studying the Bible is not focused on information, but on transformation. Here's where we intentionally focus on today by looking at different "Views" that relate to contemporary life.

One reason for doing Bible study this way is to learn *how* to study the Bible. As your group works through text, context, and what's next, you will be learning an important skill for a lifetime of encountering God's Word.

The real joy in engaging this Living Word is its power to change our lives—for the better. You don't have to get "right" answers; you do have to be open and searching—and the Spirit will lead you.

Visit **www.ileadyouth.com/3V** for

⋄ student-leader helps
⋄ background on the Gospels
⋄ worship suggestions
⋄ contents of the other studies in the 3V series

Leading the Studies

Adult and Student Leaders

Adults or high school students can lead or co-lead these studies. Interested students can facilitate the whole study or lead a particular discussion or activity for their peers. By using small groups at particular points, all students will gain more experience as both leaders and participants.

Students who have been student-leaders for *Synago* are especially qualified to lead all or portions of these 3V Bible Studies. Go to *www.ileadyouth.com* for student-leader helps and for more information about *Synago* for senior highs.

Activities

As you lead, don't hesitate to try some of the more active ideas (roleplay or drawing, for example). Sometimes the physical and verbal cues of a one-minute roleplay lead to great new insights. Another reason to try the activities is that different people learn in different ways. So expand the opportunities for everyone to learn.

Group Size

All size groups of senior highs can easily use this study method. If your group is small, do most of the sections together, with occasional conversations in pairs or threes. If the group is larger, break into small groups or pairs more often, with times of reporting and talking as a whole group.

Bibles

Everyone should have access to a study book and a Bible. Have a variety of translations of the Bible available. Referring to the different translations is a helpful skill in Bible study. Sometimes subtle nuances in the wording can give more clarity or insight. Sometimes they help raise good questions.

The New Revised Standard Version (NRSV) is printed here so that students can feel good about writing in their books. They can highlight words and phrases they think are important or note questions that the Scripture passage raises for them, which they might not do in a Bible.

Fitting Your Time

This approach to Bible study is very flexible. You may choose to:

- **Do all of a particular study or streamline it;**
- **Do the study in one session or over two or three;**
- **Do all the questions, or choose some;**
- **Do some of the studies or all of them.**

If you need to spend less time, plan to do What's the Text? and What's the Context? You may wish to deal with fewer of the questions in each section. Be sure to do After Looking at Both the Text and the Context.

If you have more time, add View You (U) in What's Next? If you have still more time, use one or all of the other Views (A, B, C) for some spirited debate.

Suggested Schedule Options

One Session Only

5–10 minutes	What's the Text?
20–25	What's the Context? (Selected Questions)
20–35	What's Next? (Selected Views)
5–10	View You

Two Sessions

10–15 minutes	What's the Text?
20–30	What's the Context? (Selected Questions)
10–15	What's Next (One View)
10–15 minutes	Review of Text and Context
30–40	What's Next? (Remaining Views)
5–10	View You

Three Sessions

1. Do What's the Text? and What's the Context? (Most Questions)
2. Do a review of Text and Context; finish any remaining Context sections and After Looking at Both the Text and the Context.
3. Do a brief review of previous sessions; choose one or more of the Views in What's Next? Close with View U. Consider using the Worship Suggestions from *www.ileadyouth.com/3V.*

The Reluctant Judge

Judges 6:11-17

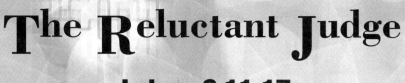

Have you ever been asked to do something for which you felt completely unprepared? Take a new subject at school? Play an unfamiliar position on a sports team? Assume a big responsibility at church? It can feel overwhelming. "Why me?" you think. "Couldn't someone else do this job?" That's what Gideon thought, too, until God showed him how we all depend on God—not on ourselves—most of all.

2

¹¹ Now the angel of the LORD came and sat under the oak at Ophrah, which belonged to Joash the Abiezrite, as his son Gideon was beating out wheat in the wine press, to hide it from the Midianites. ¹² The angel of the LORD appeared to him and said to him, "The LORD is with you, you mighty warrior." ¹³ Gideon answered him, "But sir, if the LORD is with us, why then has all this happened to us? And where are all his wonderful deeds that our ancestors recounted to us, saying, 'Did not the LORD bring us up from Egypt?' But now the LORD has cast us off, and given us into the hand of Midian." ¹⁴ Then the LORD turned to him and said, "Go in this might of yours and deliver Israel from the hand of Midian; I hereby commission you." ¹⁵ He responded, "But sir, how can I deliver Israel? My clan is the weakest in Manasseh, and I am the least in my family." ¹⁶ The LORD said to him, "But I will be with you, and you shall strike down the Midianites, every one of them." ¹⁷ Then he said to him, "If now I have found favor with you, then show me a sign that it is you who speak with me."

Judges 6:11-17

Read the passage aloud. Have others read silently from other translations and report any differences in the wording.

• How do the differences help you understand the text?

• What questions do the differences raise for you?

Highlight words or phrases in the text that you think are important. List any questions the text raises for you.

Imagine that God has called you to be a leader in some effort by your church or your community—a ministry of food to the homeless, for example.

• How would you respond?

• What excuses would you make?

• What tests would you ask God to perform to show that your calling was real?

• What new insights did you gain into Gideon's story?

Discuss as a group your answers to these questions.

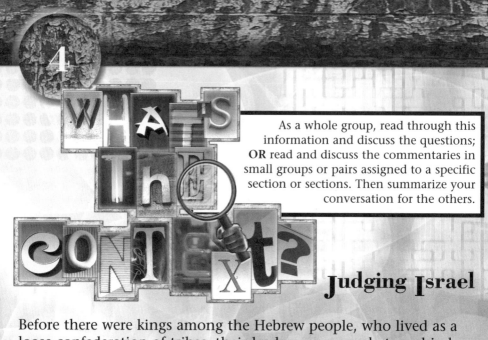

4

WHAT'S THE CONTEXT?

As a whole group, read through this information and discuss the questions; **OR** read and discuss the commentaries in small groups or pairs assigned to a specific section or sections. Then summarize your conversation for the others.

Judging Israel

Before there were kings among the Hebrew people, who lived as a loose confederation of tribes, their leaders were prophets and judges. God was understood to be their king. The prophets were the religious leaders, speaking about (and sometimes for) God. The judges were military and political leaders; they didn't hear court cases the way our judges do today. Some of the judges, such as Othniel (see Judges 3:7-11), were outstanding; others, such as Samson, weren't so good (see Judges 13–16). At least one judge, Deborah, was a woman. Gideon became a judge.

• All of Israel's neighbors were ruled by kings. During the time of the judges, who was understood to be Israel's king?
• In what ways did this understanding give Israel an advantage over its neighbors?
• In what ways did people see it as a disadvantage?
• In what way was the system of judges a test of Israel's faith?

Sin, Reap the Consequences, Be Delivered, Repeat

The judges could not keep the people from blending their worship of God with the worship of local gods of the Canaanite tribes, whom they had not fully conquered and who lived nearby. In the Book of Judges you'll see a phrase repeated again and again that gives the book its shape: "The Israelites did what was evil in the sight of the LORD." The story of Gideon begins in just this way (Judges 6:1). The people committed evil. In fact, Gideon's own father kept an altar to Baal. In the story, as a consequence, the Lord allowed the Midianites to dominate the Israelites for seven years.

A pattern repeats itself throughout the book: The people do what is evil (usually, following other gods), something bad happens, the people cry out to God for help, and God raises up a judge to help things get back on God's track.

- In what ways does our own society "do what is evil in the sight of the LORD"? How do we worship other "gods"?
- How do you see God working to put things back on God's track?
- How does God work to keep your own life on God's track?
- God chose Gideon to be judge, yet Gideon was a man who lived in a household where other gods were worshiped. What does God's choice suggest to you about God? about God's relationship with human beings?

Who Are the Midianites and Why Is Gideon Afraid?

The Midianites were nomads from the deserts of Arabia on the eastern side of the Red Sea. Because their land was poor for farming, they moved around often and had to get their food from people who grew it. Instead of buying the food and supplies they needed, the Midianites had a reputation for simply stealing whatever they wanted. One of the most popular Midianite strategies was to starve their enemies by taking away the food they needed to survive. For these reasons Gideon was beating out the grain from the chaff down in a winepress, instead of doing it in an open area outside. He was hiding to keep Midianite raiders from finding his grain and taking it.

The Midianites didn't just steal food; they stole people too. They would make slaves of them or sell them into slavery to some other tribe or country. In Genesis 37:28 and 36, the caravan who buy Joseph and sell him into slavery in Egypt are Midianites.

• The Midianites and Israelites had not always been enemies. Read Exodus 18:1-27 for a story of Moses and his father-in-law. How does this text affect your view of the Midianites?
• Read Judges 6:7-10, the brief account of a prophet sent by God before the calling of Gideon. According to this text, why does God allow the Midianites to plunder the crops of Israel?

Mighty Warrior? Ha!

When God calls him to be a military and political leader of his people, Gideon is hiding from the Midianites, who had invaded and destroyed much of the Israelites' land and were now occupying it. So it seems almost comical when the angel addresses Gideon as "you mighty warrior."

Gideon tries to weasel out. Sound familiar? That's also what Moses did when God called him. Gideon lists a number of excuses: His tribe, Manasseh, is the smallest; and he is the least of his family. And Gideon doesn't think that he would make a very good judge. God offers Gideon the only assurance that any of God's chosen ever get. "I will be with you," God tells the reluctant judge. Unfortunately, Gideon feels that that God's assurance is not quite enough and asks for a sign.

- Much of the early history of the Israelite people is the story of how they slowly learned to put their trust in God. What other examples do you recall? How does Gideon's story add to that history?
- If you were in Gideon's shoes, would it be enough to know that God was with you? Why, or why not?
- Has anyone ever recognized potential in you that you had not yet seen in yourself? How did he or she tell you about it? How did you respond?
- In what ways is it exciting to learn about great potential that others see in you? In what ways can it be intimidating or frightening?

After Looking at Both the Text and the Context . . .

Deal with some or all of these questions before moving to What's Next?

- What new insights do you have?

- Which characters or events stand out for you?

- What answers did you find to the questions raised earlier?

- What new questions does the text raise?

- How is Gideon like you? How is he different?

- Who would the Midianites be today? Can you think of a any group that would compare to them in our world?

- What one learning will you take from this study and apply to your life?

Choose one or more of Views A, B, and C to discuss; **OR** have different small groups talk about one and then summarize the discussion for the other groups. **Be sure to have everyone complete View U.**

This Is a Test

Have you ever heard anyone begin a request or demand by saying, "If you really love me, you will . . . "? Have you ever said this to someone? Sometimes people even try to put God to a test in this way. They want some sign that God loves them, that they can really trust God.

Read Judges 6:36-40. Even after the angel consumes Gideon's offering with fire—a pretty impressive demonstration—Gideon doesn't seem impressed for long. He asks—not once, but twice—for God to perform a miracle. Gideon asks God to show him that he is the one through whom God will save Israel. God doesn't have to grant even one of Gideon's requests for proof but gives Gideon "his dew" both times he requests it.

- Is Gideon doubting God? Or do you think that Gideon is questioning only the idea that he (Gideon) might actually be a military leader? Explain.
- Read Matthew 4:5-7. How does Jesus respond when Satan tempts him to perform a spectacular public miracle. Why do you think Jesus responds the way he does?
- If we are not supposed to "put the Lord your God to the test," why do you think God goes along with Gideon's request?
- When and how have you ever imposed a test on God as a sign of God's love for you?
- How is it possible to turn prayer into a proof or test of God?

The Incredible Shrinking Army

Now it's time for God to test Gideon. In ancient times (and today), most people assumed that the army with the most soldiers has the better chance of winning a battle. God seems to follow the opposite approach. That's not so unusual: Throughout the Bible, God often reverses what most people expect.

Read Judges 7:1-3. Anyone who is so afraid that his hand trembles with fear is allowed to leave. There must have been a lot of trembling, because 22,000 men go home; and Gideon loses two-thirds of his army. In a way, though, this strategy makes sense; only the bravest are left to fight.

In God's opinion, however, the army is still too large. Read Judges 7:4-8. God tells Gideon to take the 10,000 men to a stream for a drink of water. Those who lap water from the stream like dogs stay with Gideon; those who kneel down and cup the water in their palms are dismissed. That leaves only 300 soldiers to fight the fearsome Midianite army.

- Why, do you think, does God intend to use such a dramatically weakened army against the Midianites? What lesson does God intend for the Israelites to learn?
- How is God putting Gideon to the test?
- When have you ever taken credit for something when someone else, instead, really deserved that credit?
- How do people today take credit for their successes, instead of giving credit to God?

 **Breaking Pots and Flashes of Light**

In recent times, the United States military has been researching the use of unpleasant noise as a weapon. Certain sounds make you want to run away (such as the music your parents like to listen to). While this research into non-violent responses to crowd control and violent situations is considered cutting-edge today, we discover from Gideon's story that using noise as a weapon is nothing new. In fact, it's more than 3,000 years old.

Read Judges 7:19-23 to learn how Gideon and his army defeat the Midianites. In the dark of night, armed with torches, clay pots, and trumpets, the army of Israel surrounds the camp of their enemy. When they hear the signal, Gideon's soldiers smash the pots and blow the trumpets. In between trumpet blows, the Israelites shout, "A sword of the LORD and Gideon!" This racket is designed to startle and confuse the Midianite army. And does it ever succeed! The Midianite soldiers run off in all directions. In the dark and confusion, some of the Midianites even attack one another.

- What, do you think, does Gideon think when God tells him the strategy for engaging this much larger and better-armed force?
- What, do you think, do the startled Midianites think when they awake to hear trumpets and see torches surrounding their camp?
- What does using noise, instead of the usual weapons, to confuse and defeat the enemy reveal about God's ways?
- What lesson, do you think, were the Israelites supposed to learn from God? How does achieving victory without weapons of warfare reinforce that lesson?

Are You Extra-Ordinary or Extraordinary?

When we first meet Gideon, he is the most ordinary guy you could imagine. There is nothing remarkable about him, except his "ordinariness." You might say that he is extra-ordinary, or more ordinary than most of us. Even when he tests God, Gideon simply proves that he is like the vast majority of human beings.

When Gideon begins to do what God asks of him, this extra-ordinary guy does some pretty extraordinary things.

- In what ways do you think God can use an ordinary (even an extra-ordinary) person like you?
- How would you respond? What would God have to "prove" to you?
- How is God calling you to something extraordinary in your life? your family? your school? your congregation?

Check *www.ileadyouth.com/3V* for worship suggestions.

Redeeming Qualities

Ruth 1:6-18

"Where you go, I will go.... Your people shall be my people." At weddings, people often read these words that Ruth spoke to Naomi. But the original words are spoken between two women, not between a bride and bridegroom. And not just between any two women: These women are not related by blood, and they are from different countries with different religions. On top of that, Naomi doesn't even think that Ruth, her foreign daughter-in-law, should come with her. Ruth's devotion is radical—and extraordinary.

⁶ Then [Naomi] started to return with her daughters-in-law from the country of Moab, for she had heard in the country of Moab that the Lord had considered his people and given them food. ⁷ So she set out from the place where she had been living, she and her two daughters-in-law, and they went on their way to go back to the land of Judah. ⁸ But Naomi said to her two daughters-in-law, "Go back each of you to your mother's house. May the Lord deal kindly with you, as you have dealt with the dead and with me. ⁹ The Lord grant that you may find security, each of you in the house of your husband." Then she kissed them, and they wept aloud. ¹⁰ They said to her, "No, we will return with you to your people." ¹¹ But Naomi said, "Turn back, my daughters, why will you go with me? Do I still have sons in my womb that they may become your husbands? ¹² Turn back, my daughters, go your way, for I am too old to have a husband. Even if I thought there was hope for me, even if I should have a husband tonight and bear sons, ¹³ would you then wait until they were grown? Would you then refrain from marrying? No, my daughters, it has been far more bitter for me than for you, because the hand of the Lord has turned against me." ¹⁴ Then they wept aloud again. Orpah kissed her mother-in-law, but Ruth clung to her.

¹⁵ So she said, "See, your sister-in-law has gone back to her people and to her gods; return after your sister-in-law."

^{16} But Ruth said,

> "Do not press me to leave you
>   or to turn back from following you!
> Where you go, I will go;
>   Where you lodge, I will lodge;
> your people shall be my people,
>   and your God my God.
> ^{17} Where you die, I will die—
>   there will I be buried.
> May the LORD do thus and so to me,
>   and more as well,
> if even death parts me from you!"

^{18} When Naomi saw that she was determined to go with her, she said no more to her.

Ruth 1:6-18

15

Read the passage aloud. Have others read silently from other translations and report any differences in the wording.

• How do the differences help you understand the text?

• What questions do the differences raise for you?

Highlight words or phrases in the text you think are important. List any questions the text raises for you.

Write down the names of the three women in this story: Naomi, Ruth, and Orpah. Beside each name, list what you believe are the wants, fears, and motivations for these three widows. Compare your list with those of others in your group.

• What new insights did you gain from this exercise? Add them to your list.

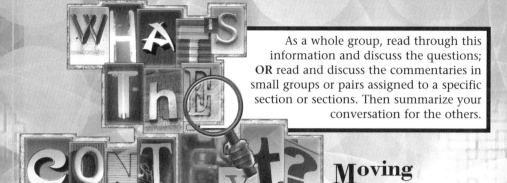

WHAT'S THE CONTEXT?

As a whole group, read through this information and discuss the questions; **OR** read and discuss the commentaries in small groups or pairs assigned to a specific section or sections. Then summarize your conversation for the others.

Moving to Moab

This text is part of a much longer story. It begins with a famine in Bethlehem, where Naomi and her family live. Because there is not enough for them to eat, they move to Moab, a country on the eastern side of the Dead Sea. (Use an Old Testament Bible map to locate Bethlehem and Moab.)

The Israelites didn't like the Moabites. They were related through Lot, Abraham's nephew; but the Moabites worshiped other gods and sometimes clashed with Israel. When you're hungry, though, you move to where the food is, regardless of who your neighbors will be.

While in Moab, Naomi's husband dies and her sons marry Moabite women. The storyteller never reveals why the sons do not return home to find wives of their own religion and tradition. Perhaps Naomi never imagined that she or her sons would return to Israel. In any case, we know that such foreign marriages were seen as turning away from God's covenant with Israel and invariably led to trouble (see the stories of Esau, Solomon, and Ahab, for example).

Ironically, of course, in this story about foreigners, it's really Naomi and her family who are the outsiders.

• How do you think Naomi felt when she was uprooted from her home in Bethlehem and had to move to Moab?

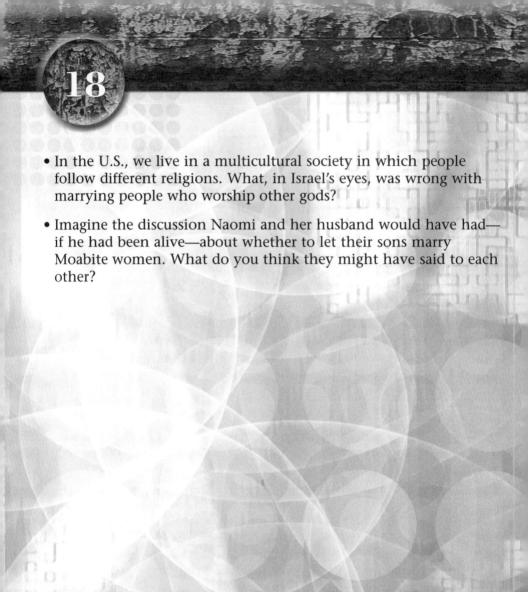

18

- In the U.S., we live in a multicultural society in which people follow different religions. What, in Israel's eyes, was wrong with marrying people who worship other gods?

- Imagine the discussion Naomi and her husband would have had—if he had been alive—about whether to let their sons marry Moabite women. What do you think they might have said to each other?

Tragedy Strikes

One of worst things that can happen to a woman in biblical times happens to Naomi. Her husband dies and leaves her a widow. She can still depend on her sons for support, though. That's one reason why people in ancient societies believed that having male children was so important. Then both of her sons die, leaving Naomi without support and leaving her daughters-in-law, Orpah and Ruth, widows.

Orpah and Ruth are young enough to remarry. But Naomi now feels the full burden of being a foreigner in Moab. She decides to go home, where the famine has now ended; and she advises Orpah and Ruth to remain in Moab to find new husbands. Naomi fears that in Israel her foreign daughters-in-law will not be accepted. By begging Ruth and Orpah not to accompany her, Naomi is acting in what she believes is the best interest of the younger women.

- Ruth is not bound either by law or custom to stay with or support her mother-in-law after her husband dies. How does knowing this add to your understanding of Ruth's decision to accompany Naomi?
- In Hebrew, the name *Naomi* means "sweet" or "pleasant." When she returns to Bethlehem, she tells people to call her "Mara" from now on—a name that means "bitter." Read Ruth 1:19-21. How would you describe Naomi's feelings about her past? her future?
- What could make Ruth want to go with her mother-in-law when Naomi is clearly trying to get Ruth to stay in her own homeland for her own good?

Old Testament Welfare and Redemption

After Ruth follows Naomi to Bethlehem, she participates in the Israelite version of welfare, called *gleaning*. According to the books of the Law, a farmer could go through his field only once to harvest grain. In addition, he had to leave a portion of the field completely unharvested. The grain that the reapers missed or intentionally left standing was reserved for the poor, who could go along behind the harvesters and pick up, or "glean," whatever remained.

Ruth is gleaning grain so that she and Naomi can bake bread. But then she happens to catch Boaz's eye. As a relative of Naomi's late husband, Boaz has a right to "redeem" the land Naomi's husband gave up when she and her family went to Moab. Redemption allowed people to keep land in their extended families.

In a romantic and somewhat scandalous episode, Naomi and Ruth scheme to lead Boaz to exercise this traditional right. By redeeming the land, Boaz acquires Ruth the Moabite and inherits the responsibility to care for Naomi. Read Ruth 3:1–4:6 to learn this part of the story.

- As the ancient Hebrew people understood the Law, to whom did the grain in the fields ultimately belong? Why?
- How does this understanding compare with modern views of property ownership?
- Would it be possible to have gleaning laws today? Explain.
- Have you ever experienced or do you know about gleaning practiced today?
- Why, do you think, does Boaz choose to take responsibility for supporting Naomi?

Jesus' Scandalous Great-Great-Great-Great-Great-Great-Great-Great (You Get the Picture) Grandmother

Boaz and Ruth have a son named Obed, who becomes the father of Jesse, who was the father of David the king. Now read Matthew 1:1-16, which contains an account of Jesus' genealogy. Notice that Ruth is one of four women listed. It was unusual to include women in a family history like this, but it is unheard of to include women who might bring scandal to the family. (Apparently, including scandalous men was OK.)

Tamar (see Genesis 38) had a son through an incestuous relationship with her father-in-law, Judah. Rahab was a prostitute in Jericho. David committed adultery with Bathsheba. All four women also were Gentiles or were married to Gentiles.

What could be scandalous about a nice young woman like Ruth? Well, Ruth was a Moabite. According to the Law of Moses (see Deuteronomy 23:3), "No Ammonite or Moabite or any of their descendents may enter the assembly of the Lord, not even in the tenth generation" (TNIV). These laws regained special emphasis when the Jewish people returned from exile early in the sixth century B.C. Because Jewish leaders such as Ezra and Nehemiah saw the exile as God's punishment for worshiping foreign idols, the Jews who returned to Jerusalem were encouraged to end their marriages to foreigners.

• During a time of great prejudice against foreigners, why, do you think, would someone be remembered and included the story of Ruth, which had taken place 600 years earlier during the time of the Judges? What point do you think the writer was trying to make?
• How does Ruth's story suggest that God works through people outside our own faith tradition? How is this a radical idea today?
• Since King David is only three generations from his Moabite great-grandmother Ruth, and no descendant of a Moabite can enter the assembly of the Lord, does that make David an Israelite or not?

21

After Looking at Both the Text and the Context . . .

Deal with some or all of these questions before moving to What's Next?

- What new insights do you have?

- Which characters or events stand out for you?

- Have you found any answers to the questions raised earlier? What are they?

- What new questions does the text raise for you?

- In what ways do you identify with Naomi? with Ruth? with Orpah? with Boaz?

- What one learning will you take from this study and apply to your life?

Choose one or more of
Views A, B, and C to discuss;
OR have different small
groups talk about one and
then summarize the
discussion for the other
groups. **Be sure to have
everyone complete View U.**

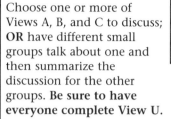 

View A — Just Deal With It

Naomi and her husband have to make a drastic change in their lives
when famine comes to their homeland. They leave their family, their
home, and all that is familiar and move to a foreign country. There
they make a new life among strangers, two of whom eventually
become part of their family as daughters-in-law.

• What does Naomi's allowing her sons to marry local women
  indicate about the family's life in Moab?
• Have you ever had to make a drastic change in your life because of
  circumstances beyond your control?
• Have you ever moved to a new place, among people who were
  strangers? If so, how did you adapt to customs that were different
  from your own? How did you learn to blend in to the community?
  What was it like to give up some of your old ways of doing things?

Naomi finds herself in a difficult situation. She has to deal with the
deaths of her husband and her sons. She responds to her situation
by returning to Bethlehem.

• What feelings do you think motivate Naomi's decision to return
  home?
• Have there been events in your life that you could not have
  prevented that have left you in a difficult situation? If so, how did
  you deal with them?

Making Good Choices

Ruth and Orpah have every reason to take Naomi's advice and stay in Moab. After all, they know the language and customs and have family and friends there. In Israel, they would have only their mother-in-law. So Orpah stays. But Ruth is determined to go to Israel. By staying with Naomi, Ruth chooses this foreign woman over her own people—and chooses Naomi's God over the gods of her homeland.

- What might motivate Naomi's desire for Ruth to stay behind?
- What—other than the love she has for her mother-in-law—might motivate Ruth's desire to go with Naomi?
- Do you think that Ruth has any idea what she is getting into by going with Naomi? Explain.
- Do you think that Orpah makes a bad choice?
- Why, do you think, does the author of the story uphold Ruth's choice as a good one?
- If you were Ruth, what would you have done?
- How significant is it that part of Ruth's choice to live in Israel means that she will worship the God of Israel?
- What does Ruth's story, written down in a time of hostility to foreigners and foreign gods, suggest about the nature of the God of Israel?

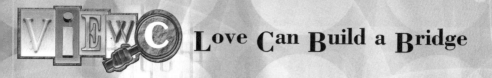

Love Can Build a Bridge

Ruth's love for Naomi builds a bridge between the two women and allows Ruth to take the risky step of leaving her home, family, and gods to embrace Naomi's home, family, and God. Love builds another bridge in this story, a bridge between Ruth and Boaz. When Boaz hears of her kindness to Naomi, he welcomes Ruth to eat with his workers; he asks them to watch after her. Then Boaz goes about "redeeming" the property of Naomi's late husband, taking Naomi into his household, and marrying Ruth.

- In what way is Ruth "redeemed" in this story? How is Naomi redeemed?
- Boaz could have married Ruth without redeeming his kinsman's property and taking on the responsibility of providing support for Naomi. But Ruth asks him to do it, and he does. What does the story suggest to you about Ruth's character? about Boaz's character?
- In what way does Boaz take a risk in marrying a Moabite woman? Why, do you think, does he do it?
- What qualities, do you think, might Boaz have seen in Ruth that would make him disregard the fact that she is a foreign woman?

Wanted: More Ruths

Ruth demonstrates her commitment and love for her mother-in-law by following her to Bethlehem and by working to support her. Boaz shows his love and commitment to Ruth by seeing that she and Naomi are cared for. Jesus says that when we help someone in need, we are helping him.

- Have you ever arrived in a new place (neighborhood, school, church, youth group) and been made to feel particularly welcome? How did that welcome change your feelings about being in a new situation?
- How might you help those who are new to your neighborhood, school, church, or youth group feel welcome?

This week, consider who might be a "Naomi" in your life, someone who is in a difficult situation or feeling "bitter" or down and could use someone to stand by him or her. Prayerfully ask God to lead you to be a "Ruth" to that person.

Check *www.ileadyouth.com/3V*
for worship suggestions.

Prayer Makes the Ordinary Extraordinary

1 Samuel 1:3-11

Have you ever felt left out or rejected? Perhaps someone poked fun at you because of your intelligence or because you couldn't throw a football. Looking back on the situation, you can remember how much those actions hurt your feelings and how no one could really help you feel better about yourself. You may not even remember how you recovered from the pain. Hannah could relate. She felt rejected by God because she had been unable to have a baby. Hannah's prayers to God healed her pain and showed her how much God loved her. Her faith changed her life from the ordinary to extraordinary.

3 Now [Elkanah] used to go up year by year from his town to worship and to sacrifice to the LORD of hosts at Shiloh, where the two sons of Eli, Hophni and Phinehas, were priests of the LORD. 4 On the day when Elkanah sacrificed, he would give portions to his wife Peninnah and to all her sons and daughters; 5 but to Hannah he gave a double portion, because he loved her, though the LORD had closed her womb. 6 Her rival [Peninnah] used to provoke her severely, to irritate her, because the LORD had closed her womb. 7 So it went on year by year; as often as she went up to the house of the LORD, she used to provoke her. Therefore Hannah wept and would not eat. 8 Her husband Elkanah said to her, "Hannah, why do you weep? Why do you not eat? Why is your heart sad? Am I not more to you than ten sons?"

9 After they had eaten and drunk at Shiloh, Hannah rose and presented herself before the LORD. Now Eli the priest was sitting on the seat beside the doorpost of the temple of the LORD. 10 She was deeply distressed and prayed to the LORD and wept bitterly. 11 She made this vow: "O LORD of hosts, if only you will look on the misery of your servant, and remember me, and not forget your servant, but will give to your servant a male child, then I will set him before you as a nazirite until the day of his death. He shall drink neither wine nor intoxicants, and no razor shall touch his head."

1 Samuel 1:3-11

Read the passage aloud. Have others read silently from other translations and report any differences in the wording.

• How do the differences help you understand the text?

• What questions do the differences raise for you?

Highlight words or phrases in the text you think are important. List any questions the text raises for you.

Write a summary of this story in three to five sentences. What issues does Hannah face? Who tries to help her?

• What new insights did you gain? Add them to your list.

Using contemporary language, create a skit reenacting the scene at Shiloh (1 Samuel 3-11) between Elkanah, Hannah, and Peninnah.

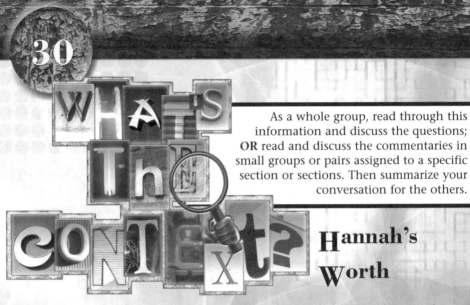

WHAT'S THE CONTEXT?

Hannah's Worth

As a whole group, read through this information and discuss the questions; **OR** read and discuss the commentaries in small groups or pairs assigned to a specific section or sections. Then summarize your conversation for the others.

First Samuel is devoted largely to the stories of the first kings of Israel, Saul and David. However, the book is named for the boy who became a prophet and judge over Israel. Samuel did more than foretell the future; he was a spokesman for God. Many scholars believe that Samuel may have written the first twenty-five chapters of this book.

This story makes clear that the extraordinary nature of Samuel's life of faithfulness to God begins with the extraordinary faith of his mother, Hannah, who had been unable to have children. To the people of Hannah's day (3,000 years ago), barrenness was a sign that a woman was out of favor with God. Barren women had little value to their families.

Yet Elkanah, Hannah's husband, still holds Hannah in special regard. He seems to love her more than he loves his other wife, Peninnah.

- Does knowing that Samuel may have written at least the first twenty-five chapters of this book make Hannah's story more compelling? Why, or why not?
- Given the prevailing views of women and their role in biblical society, how does Elkanah's attitude seem unusual? What clues do you find in the text that he loved Hannah more than Peninnah? What does Elkanah's attitude suggest about God's attitude toward us?
- How does this story contrast society's view of what makes a person extraordinary with God's view?

The Other Woman

Elkanah was one of many husbands in the Old Testament who had more than one wife. Elkanah probably married Peninnah because Hannah proved unable to have children. For husbands, having more than one wife was a way to have more children, especially sons, who could extend their clan and carry on their father's legacy.

Although polygamy was legal, it often created conflict. There were jealousies in Abraham's family (see Genesis 21) and Jacob's family (Genesis 30). The text even describes Hannah and Peninnah as rivals.

- Why was Hannah jealous of Peninnah? Why was Peninnah jealous of Hannah?
- How did Peninnah express her jealousy? How did Hannah react? What do the differences in their actions reveal about the two women?
- In a culture in which women were valued largely for their ability to produce children, why, do you think, did Elkanah continue to love Hannah so much?
- How, do you think, did Hannah feel about Elkanah's marriage to Peninnah?

Am I Not Enough?

Her infertility, combined with the taunts of Peninnah, appears to have emotionally crushed Hannah. Today, we would probably diagnose her condition as depression. She is sad all of the time and doesn't want to eat. She probably lost weight and slept a lot because she lacked energy. Deep in depression, Hannah could not feel the affirming love of her husband.

Depression, some psychologists say, is anger turned inward. People who become deeply depressed may think of themselves as losers. No matter how much people try to tell them otherwise, nothing can shake their feelings of worthlessness, just as Elkanah's efforts fail to console Hannah.

- Why would Hannah be angry? How has she turned that anger inward?
- Why, do you think, does Hannah allow Peninnah to abuse her emotionally with insults?
- To what extent, do you think, does Hannah begin to accept Peninnah's definition of her, instead of defining herself?
- Have you ever known someone who was deeply depressed? How did his or her actions remind you of Hannah? How did you or others try to help? How did the person react? How did the other person's depression affect you?
- How, do you think, did Elkanah feel about Hannah's depression? Rejected? Powerless? Guilty?
- Write down a piece of advice for Hannah. How, do you think, would she have responded?

Hannah's Prayer

At the shrine at Shiloh—one of the major places of worship in ancient Israel before the building of the Temple—Hannah commits an extraordinary act. She goes to pray without her husband and, apparently, without his permission. Only a male had authority to present himself to God alone. Hannah's daring is a testimony to her faith and her commitment.

When Hannah prays, she cries and talks out loud to God. She asks God for three things: to look upon her misery (healing), to remember her (comfort), and to give her a male child (a blessing). Before she makes these requests, she first acknowledges God ("O Lord of Hosts"). She closes with a promise. If God gives her a child, she will give the child back.

- How does Hannah's prayer demonstrate faith? Read Hebrews 11:1. How does this definition of *faith* affect your answer? How does faith make the ordinary extraordinary?
- Read Matthew 6:8-13. Compare the structure of the Lord's Prayer with Hannah's prayer.
- How do you think people in your church would react if they overheard someone voicing a prayer like Hannah's? How would the person be perceived?
- Read 1 Samuel 1:12-18. How does Eli respond at first to Hannah's prayer? Why might he have responded in that way?
- What convinces Eli of Hannah's sincerity? How does Eli know that God plans to grant her request?
- How does Hannah show her faith in God's promise to her?

Hannah's Promise

Reread Hannah's prayer (verse 11). It's a reminder that children belong to God and that mothers are only temporary caregivers. Hannah promises God that her son will be a nazirite, one whose life is dedicated to the service of God. As a nazirite, Samuel could not touch anything dead, cut his hair, or have any contact with the fruit of the vine or drink any wine. These restrictions were meant to keep Samuel separated for holy living and service to God. (See Numbers 6:1-20 for the description of the nazirite vow.)

- Why, do you think, did Hannah add this promise to her request for a child? Why does she need to verbalize to God her intentions for the child? Have you ever asked your parents for something and added a promise? If so, does it affect your answer to the original question?
- Do you think that God would have granted Hannah's request without this promise? Why, or why not?
- What is Hannah's role in ensuring that Samuel remains a nazirite until death? What is Samuel's role?
- How does being a nazirite equate to holy living? How are we to live holy—to separate ourselves for service to God today?

Read 1 Samuel 2:1-4.

When Hannah brings Samuel to Eli (probably at age 2 or 3, after he has been weaned), she offers a prayer of thanksgiving to God. The song is very similar to the one Mary offers when she learns from the angel that she is to give birth to Jesus. Read this song, also called the "Magnificat," in Luke 1:46-55.

- How are the two songs similar?
- How does comparing the songs of these two mothers give you new insight into Samuel's mission? into Jesus' mission?

After Looking at Both
the Text and the Context . . .

**Deal with some or all of these questions
before moving to What's Next?**

- What new insights do you have?

- How important is prayer in dealing with challenging situations and people?

- What role does prayer play in helping us realize how extraordinary we are as children of God?

- What is the relationship between trust and prayer?

- What does this text suggest to you about the nature of marriage?

- How does Hannah's sacrifice of Samuel compare to God's sacrifice of Jesus?

- What learning from this text will you apply to your daily life?

36

Choose one or more of Views A, B, and C to discuss; **OR** have different small groups talk about one and then summarize the discussion for the other groups. **Be sure to have everyone complete View U.**

VIEW A Faith and Suffering

Hannah envies Peninnah. Yet Peninnah covets the affection from Elkanah that Hannah enjoys. Peninnah deals with her envy by hurting Hannah. Hannah allows her pain to fester into depression. Both of these women are more focused on their problems than on the problem solver, God.

But when Hannah shifts her focus from depression to deliverance, something extraordinary happens. She allows God's plan and purpose to take center stage in her life, and her prayer makes clear that her wish for a son is not simply about her desire for self-fulfillment but for fulfillment through serving God. When she gives birth to Samuel and then gives the boy to Eli to raise, Hannah is affirmed not just as a woman and a person of worth but as an example of faith for all of Israel.

- In what ways do you feel barrenness in your spiritual life?
- What things do you want to "birth" in your spiritual life?
- What does "Hannah-faith" mean to you?
- Recall any of your own encounters with suffering from which God has delivered you or others. How do these experiences compare with Hannah's? What role has faith and prayer played in this deliverance?
- Read John 9:1-7. How does Jesus address the question of why people suffer? How does his answer relate to the story of Hannah's suffering for so many years?

VIEW B A Discouraging Word

Words have great power. A discouraging word from one of our peers can be devastating, especially if that word calls attention to ways in which we're different from the others in the group. It can affect how we view ourselves; the way we dress, talk, and think. Peninnah's taunts seem to reinforce Hannah's negative view of herself.

But an encouraging word can make all the difference to someone who is struggling with low self-esteem. Read 1 Samuel 1:12-18. Notice how Hannah's whole outlook changes after Eli encourages her.

Many teenagers struggle with a negative self-image. During the teen years especially, we worry about how well we are accepted by our peers. We want to fit in. Some teens, acting like Peninnah, use words as weapons to attack their rivals and reinforce their own status within the group. Teens on the receiving end of such words may react like Hannah, thinking of themselves as losers and social misfits. They may lose sight of how God views them: as children of worth, made in God's own image.

- Think of persons you know whom others consider to be "social misfits." How could this story address their situations?
- How can criticism cripple? How can it strengthen?
- Read Ephesians 4:25–5:1. What encouraging word will you give to build up someone who has a poor self-image?
- Read 1 Peter 2:9. When Peter wrote this Scripture, being a Christian was not a social norm. What does this Scripture say to you about being a Christian in the twenty-first century?
- How does Hannah's promise to raise Samuel as a nazirite, holy and set apart, address this issue?

38

Deliverance and Depression

Depression affects persons of all ages, including young people. Research shows that one in five children have either a mental, behavioral, or emotional problem. Among teenagers, one in eight may suffer from depression. Only about thirty percent of these teens with depression receive intervention or treatment, while the rest struggle through the pain and hurt through adulthood and are at much greater risk for suicide or winding up in the criminal justice system.

Many of the high school shootings that have taken place across America resulted from undetected and untreated depression. Many of the juveniles who have perpetrated these crimes (and other types of violence) have been diagnosed with depression, much of which has resulted from unhealthy peer relationships, bullying, and ridiculing.

- How can we as Christian witnesses address the rising incidence of depression among children and adolescents?
- What are issues affecting teenagers that make them depressed? How can you help address these concerns?
- What could you say to a person with suicidal feelings? to someone who threatens violence against a peer? to someone who feels rejected at school?
- How can parents help address these issues?
- How do Hannah decision to pray and Eli's reaction to her prayers address the rising number of depressed teenagers who turn to violence and suicide as an answer?

A note about suicide: If a friend or family member talks about suicide or expresses such feelings, take him or her seriously. Get help. Even if the friend has "sworn" you to secrecy, talk to an adult about intervening.

VIEW U · Prayer Changes Things

Prayer enables Hannah to fulfill her divine purpose in God. At the beginning of this story, Hannah feels depressed, unworthy, and rejected; she goes to Shiloh as an observer, not as a worshiper. The story ends with Hannah going to Shiloh as a worshiper, feeling empowered and affirmed. Hannah's prayers—and God's answer—give her a reason to live. Prayer changes things.

On this page or on a separate sheet of paper, briefly describe a way in which prayer has changed your life; or list areas in which would you like prayer to make a difference, such as:

• Family
• Self-esteem
• School
• Church life
• Career or vocational objectives
• Relationships with friends

Check *www.ileadyouth.com/3V* for worship suggestions.

39

Being King Has Its Ups and Downs

1 Samuel 10:20-27

Good news: You've just been told that you are to be the ruler of a nation. Bad news: You don't really want the job. What would you do? Give it a shot and try your best? Or run and hide? What if you were king but still had to answer to someone even higher up? That's the predicament of Saul, the first king of Israel.

²⁰ Then Samuel brought all the tribes of Israel near, and the tribe of Benjamin was taken by lot. ²¹ He brought the tribe of Benjamin near by its families, and the family of the Matrites was taken by lot. Finally he brought the family of the Matrites near man by man, and Saul the son of Kish was taken by lot. But when they sought him, he could not be found. ²² So they inquired again of the LORD, "Did the man come here?" and the LORD said, "See, he has hidden himself among the

baggage." ²³ Then they ran and brought him from there. When he took his stand among the people, he was head and shoulders taller than any of them. ²⁴ Samuel said to all the people, "Do you see the one whom the LORD has chosen? There is no one like him among all the people." And all the people shouted, "Long live the king!"

²⁵ Samuel told the people the rights and duties of the kingship; and he wrote them in a book and laid it up before the LORD. Then Samuel sent all the people back to their homes. ²⁶ Saul also went to his home at Gibeah, and with him went warriors whose hearts God had touched. ²⁷ But some worthless fellows said, "How can this man save us?" They despised him and brought him no present. But he held his peace.

1 Samuel 10:20-27

41

Read the passage aloud. Have others read silently from different translations and report any differences in the wording.

• How do the differences help you understand the text?

• What questions do the differences raise for you?

Highlight words or phrases in the text that you think are important. List any questions the text raises for you.

Imagine that you are attending a news conference where the new king, Saul, was presented by Samuel. Assign one person in your group to portray Saul and another to play Samuel. Ask others to be reporters. Stage an impromptu drama in which the reporters ask Saul and Samuel questions (such as "How Saul was chosen?" and "Why did Saul hide?").

• What new insights did you gain from this exercise? (Add them to your list.)

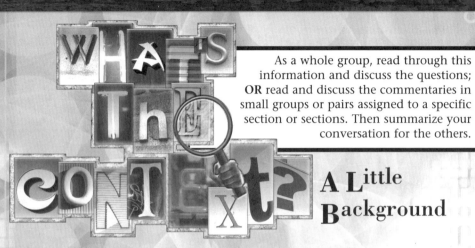

As a whole group, read through this information and discuss the questions; **OR** read and discuss the commentaries in small groups or pairs assigned to a specific section or sections. Then summarize your conversation for the others.

A Little Background

To appreciate the story of King Saul, we need to review some of the history leading up to his reign. Recall that the people of Israel were slaves in Egypt at the time of the birth of Moses (Exodus 1 and 2). Now read Exodus 3:7-9.

- Why did God decide to deliver the people from their slavery?
- Read Exodus 13:17-22. According to Scripture, who led the people out of Egypt?

The Israelites understood that God had freed them from slavery. Moses was an instrument of God, but God was a constant presence for the people. During the years in the wilderness, God led the people as a pillar of cloud and flame and was present in the tabernacle as they worshiped (see Exodus 40:34-38). Once in Israel, the people divided the land that they conquered among the tribes of Israel.

Skim over Joshua 13–21 for a description of how the land was divided. Consult a Bible map showing the locations of the various tribal areas in Israel before the time of the monarchy.

- Whom did the Israelites regard as their king?
- How did that belief set the people of Israel apart from their neighbors?

The Rule of the Judges

When the Israelites settled in Canaan, they had no central government for about 200 years. They lived as a loose confederation of tribes. During times of crisis, leaders arose who unified all or most of the tribes. Their stories are recounted in the Book of Judges.

• Read Judges 2:11-22. Why were judges necessary?

Take some time as a group to skim through the Book of Judges.

• Make a list of the judges of Israel. How many of the names do you recognize?

Read or recall (from Study 1 of this book) the story of the call of Gideon (Judges 6:11-40).

• How did Gideon become a judge?
• Would Gideon's test convince you that it was God speaking?
• How would you have reacted had you been in Gideon's position? Would you have demanded proof from God? If so, what test would you have proposed?

A constant refrain in the Book of Judges is that the "people did what was evil in the sight of the LORD" (worshiping other gods). Look through the book and see how many times you can find that phrase.

• Why do you suppose the people worshiped other gods after God raised up someone to lead them out of trouble?
• In what ways do people today do "what is evil" in God's sight? In what ways do we worship other gods?

We Want a King!

Samuel was the last of the great judges of Israel. Skim through 1 Samuel 1–3 (or review Study 3 of this book) for the story of Samuel's birth and calling.

The judges were called to serve by God. While they led the people in times of crises, the people understood themselves as being under the rule of God. Read 1 Samuel 8 as a group.

- How had Samuel's sons become judges of Israel? Why were the people unhappy with them?
- What reasons do the people give Samuel for wanting a king? Do you agree or disagree with their reasoning? Why?
- What warning does Samuel give to the people about having a king? To what extent do those warnings apply to governments today?

45

Saul Is Anointed King (in private)

God grants the request of the people. Samuel learns that he will receive instructions about whom to anoint as king over Israel. Anointing was a means often used in the ancient Middle East to honor someone or to indicate divine favor. People would also anoint themselves with scented oil for festive occasions. Scripture describes holy monuments being anointed (Genesis 28:18 and 31:13), priests being anointed (Exodus 28:41), and kings being anointed (1 Kings 1:39). *Messiah* means "the Lord's anointed" and is one of the titles used to refer to Jesus.

In 1 Samuel 9, Saul goes on an errand in search of some donkeys that have wandered off. In the course of that journey, he meets Samuel. God tells Samuel that Saul is the person who is to be anointed king. Samuel anoints Saul king in private. Read 1 Samuel 10:1-16.

- Why, do you think, does Samuel first anoint Saul king in private?
- Why, do you think, does Saul keep quiet about being anointed king?

As the study text (page 41) opens, Samuel prophesies, that is, he speaks for the Lord.

- What does Samuel tell the people about God's view of their desire for a king?
- If you had been in the crowd, how do you think the Lord's words would have made you feel? How would you have felt had you been Saul and heard those words?

Saul Is Anointed King (in Public)

Although Samuel already knows God's choice, he has the people cast lots (like drawing straws or setting up a lottery) to reveal whom God has picked as king. Using lots to determine the will of God is a fairly common practice in Scripture. After the Israelites conquered Canaan, lots were used to determine how the land would be apportioned among the tribes (Numbers 26:2). When the people returned from exile in Babylon, lots were used to select which people would live in Jerusalem (Nehemiah 11:1). Even in the New Testament, lots were used to select a new disciple to replace Judas (Acts 1:26).

• Why, do you think, does Saul allow the lottery? Why doesn't he simply announce that God has already chosen Saul and that he has been anointed king?

When the lot falls to Saul and Samuel seeks to anoint him publicly, there's one problem: They can't find him.

• Where is Saul? What do his actions suggest about his attitude toward being king?
• What would be going through your mind if you were Saul?
• Read and discuss 1 Samuel 10:27. How confident would you be about the selection of a ruler through the casting of lots?
• What qualities of Saul do you think would help make him an effective king? Which would make him an ineffective king?

47

Saul as King

The reign of Saul is described primarily as a series of battles against the historic enemies of Israel, including the Philistines and the Amorites. (Use a Bible map to locate the lands of these enemies in relation to Israel.) Overall, Saul is a successful military leader. Yet according to Scripture, he falls out of favor with God because he fails to obey God's Word. In small groups, look at 1 Samuel 13:7-14 and 1 Samuel 15:10-29.

• What was Saul commanded to do?
• What did he do?
• What appear to be his reasons for his decision?
• What do you think of the judgment that was pronounced for his alleged disobedience? Was it fair or unfair?

David and Jonathan, Saul's son, were close friends. After slaying the Philistine giant, Goliath, David serves in Saul's court. When Saul falls out of favor with God, Samuel secretly anoints David as king. Although Saul tries to kill David and the forces of Saul and David fight each other, David twice spares the life of Saul when he could have killed him (see 1 Samuel 24:1-7 and 26:1-12).

• According to the text, why does David refrain from killing Saul?
• What does this suggest to you about David? about David's fitness to be king?

After Saul and Jonathan die in battle against the Philistines, David mourns them (see 2 Samuel 1).

After Looking at Both the Text and the Context . . .

Deal with some or all of these questions
before moving to What's Next?

- What new insights do you have?

- What stands out in the story to you now?

- What answers did you find to questions you raised earlier?

- What new question do you have?

- A common quotation is "Absolute power corrupts absolutely" (Lord Acton, a British historian, 1887). How might that apply to Saul?

- What one learning will you take from this Scripture and apply to your life?

50

Choose one or more of Views A, B, and C to discuss; **OR** have different small groups talk about one and then summarize the discussion for the other groups. **Be sure to have everyone complete View U.**

The Lord Wants You

During World War I, American artist James Montgomery Flagg painted a poster depicting a man in a red, white, and blue outfit, pointing his finger directly at the viewer. The caption read, "Uncle Sam Wants You!" Although it was a call for people to enlist in the armed forces of the United States, to some the poster conveyed a sense that there was no choice. That was certainly the situation Saul faced. He was not asked by Samuel (or God) whether he wanted to be king. He was told, "The Lord wants you!"

• Do you think that Saul could have refused to serve? Why, or why not?

• Pretend you are Saul. What thoughts run through your mind as Samuel privately anoints you king? as you are hiding in the baggage?

• What would be your reasons for refusing to serve as king? What would be your reasons for accepting the job?

• Has anyone ever told you that you should pursue a career that doesn't interest you? How did you respond?

• Do you have a sense that God is calling you to some task that makes you feel uncomfortable or that frightens you?

• Do you think that God chooses courses for our lives over which we have no choice? Explain.

 **Separation of Religion and State**

Some countries have governments with close ties to religion; they may even go so far as to sponsor an official "state" religion. Others, like the United States, enshrine into law the idea that, while individuals can follow a religion of their choosing (or follow no religion), the federal government should not endorse a particular religion. Ancient Israel, on the other hand, was a theocracy, a government subject to religious authority. There was one state religion, and leaders believed that the fate of their nation depended upon everyone following it.

- Discuss the stated position of your national government toward affiliation with religion or separation from religion. What seem to be the pros and cons of the position?
- Should the conduct of those who hold public office be influenced by their religious beliefs? Why, or why not? What if their beliefs conflict with their government's policies? Would your answer change if the office holder's religious convictions differed from yours?
- Do you think that it is appropriate for ordinary citizens to advocate for policies and laws based upon their personal religious convictions? Would your answer change if your religious tradition represented a minority of citizens?

VIEW C Deciding What God Wants

The study text opens with a statement from Samuel, speaking on behalf of the Lord, telling the people what God has to say about human kings. Review 1 Samuel 10:17-19.

• How did the people know that Samuel spoke for the Lord?

We live in an information age, where anyone might make statements that could be read or heard by almost every other person on the planet. Some of these people, both famous and otherwise, claim to either speak on God's behalf or in accordance with God's will.

• How do you determine whether people are acting through God's will when they speak?
• Make a list of people you know, people in the news, or people who have made public statements (for instance, on websites or blogs) to the effect that they are acting in accordance with the will of God.
• Discuss each entry on your list and determine whether the group believes that the person is sincere and whether the person is truly motivated by the love of God and is acting in accordance with God's will.
• Can someone sincerely believe that he or she is acting in accordance with God's will but be mistaken? Explain.

VIEW U Discerning and Living God's Will

Spend some time this week reading the newspaper and watching the news. Pay particular attention to the statements of officials in the government. Whether or not these persons state that they are acting in accordance with their understanding of God, pray for them. Pray for help in discerning God's will about the situations they described.

Pray also about those things you do and say each day, and review the day's events before you go to bed. Do you think that you have acted in accordance with God's will? Pray that you might know God's will and have the courage to act upon what you come to understand. Ask for forgiveness for things you have done that have hurt others.

Check *www.ileadyouth.com/3V* for worship suggestions.

53

Convicted by the Spirit

2 Kings 23:21-25

Have you ever been convicted? Not by a judge, but by the Holy Spirit? For Christians, "conviction" comes when a person feels the full weight of disobedience to God, the full weight of sin. We view conviction as a gift of the Spirit because we cannot really turn to God in our hearts unless we see our sin and understand our need for God. Conviction can cause people to turn their lives around and try to live in accordance with God's will. And those people whose lives are changed affect those around them. When the convicted person is the ruler of a nation, as Josiah was, even bigger things happen.

²¹ The king commanded all the people, "Keep the passover to the LORD your God as prescribed in this book of the covenant." ²² No such passover had been kept since the days of the judges who judged Israel, or during all the days of the kings of Israel or of the kings of Judah; ²³ but in the eighteenth year of King Josiah this passover was kept to the LORD in Jerusalem.

²⁴ Moreover Josiah put away the mediums, wizards, teraphim, idols, and all the abominations that were seen in the land of Judah and in Jerusalem, so that he established the words of the law that were written in the book that the priest Hilkiah had found in the house of the LORD. ²⁵ Before him there was no king like him, who turned to the LORD with all his heart, with all his soul, and with all his might, according to all the law of Moses; nor did any like him arise after him.

2 Kings 23:21-25

Read the passage aloud. Have others read silently from other translations and report any differences in the wording.

- How do the differences help you understand the text?

- What questions do the differences raise for you?

Highlight words or phrases in the text that you think are important. List any questions the text raises for you.

- To what "abominations" do you think the writer is referring?

- Imagine that you are a ruler who has just discovered God's Law today and are using it to measure our own society's faithfulness to God. What would you change? What practices or customs would you "put away"? Make a list and discuss it with the group.

- What new insights did you gain from this exercise? Add them to your list.

As a whole group, read through this information and discuss the questions; OR read and discuss the commentaries in small groups or pairs assigned to a specific section or sections. Then summarize your conversation for the others.

The Sometimes Unfaithful Kings of Judah

For some background leading up to the establishment of the monarchy among the people of Israel, refer to page 43, in the study on King Saul.

Saul, David, and Solomon were the first three kings of Israel. The problem with being a king of Israel, as opposed to king of another nation, was that the king of Israel was directly answerable to God. While Israel was a nation much like other nations, its people understood that they had a special identity.

Read Exodus 19:5-6 and Deuteronomy 28:9. Discuss how these passages might be interpreted to limit the power of a king.

Saul, the first king of Israel, was considered to be disobedient to God (see page 48). Although David, Saul's successor, was generally viewed favorably in Scripture, he committed adultery with Bathsheba and conspired to have her husband killed (see 2 Samuel 11–12:25). Solomon, David's son, built the Temple of God; but he had many wives and concubines who worshiped other gods. And he had built places of worship for these other gods too. Late in his life, Solomon himself worshiped other gods (1 Kings 11:1-13).

Following Solomon's death, the kingdom of Israel split in two. The Northern Kingdom was called Israel and had its capital at Samaria. The Southern Kingdom was called Judah and

had its capital at Jerusalem (see, generally, 1 Kings 12). Jeroboam, the first king of the Northern Kingdom, Israel, did not want his subjects traveling to Jerusalem to worship God.

- Why, do you think, did Jeroboam object to his people worshiping in Jerusalem? (See 1 Kings 12:25-27.)

Jeroboam established two altars, one at Bethel and the other at Dan, where his people could sacrifice and worship God. Bethel was an ancient place of worship for the people of Israel (see Genesis 28:19). Jeroboam erected statues of calves, representing God, at both places. A prophet of Judah condemned this as idol worship (see 1 Kings 13:1-10).

- If the golden calves represented God, what was the problem? (See Exodus 20:4.)

Rehoboam was the first king of Judah. His father was Solomon, but his mother was an Ammonite. During Rehoboam's reign, the people continued to engage in idol worship (see 1 Kings 14:21-29).

Over the centuries, kings rose and fell in Judah and Israel—some with very long reigns and others with very short ones. The Scriptures say little about their reigns, except with respect to their faithfulness to the covenant with God. Skim through 1 Kings 12—2 Kings 20, and note what these Scriptures say about some of these kings.

Sins of the Father (and Grandfather)

Read about the acts of the kings of Judah and Israel, and you'll find it stunning to see how far they and the people had strayed (perhaps without even realizing it) from true obedience to God. The wrongness of some of these acts, such as when the people "went after false idols" (2 Kings 17:15), is obvious; others may require a little explanation. Here are some examples from 2 Kings 17:15-17:

- **Making a sacred pole:** Worshiping the Canaanite goddess of fertility
- **Worshiping the host of heaven:** Worshiping of the sun, moon and stars
- **Making children pass through the fire:** Sacrificial burning of children, especially of a family's first child
- **Using divination and augury:** Using natural phenomena, such as cloud patterns or flight patterns of birds, to determine what to do or to predict the future
- **Selling themselves to do evil:** Engaging in ritual prostitution involved with Baal worship

Manasseh, Josiah's grandfather, was a king of Judah whom biblical writers regarded as especially wicked. Read 2 Kings 21 and make a list of his deeds.

- Which of the evil acts in the list above did Manasseh commit?
- What acts did he commit that are not on this list?

Keep your list of Manasseh's sins to use later in this study.

59

The Boy King

Josiah was 8 years old when he became king. According to 2 Kings 22:3, it wasn't until the eighteenth year of his reign, when he was 26, that he began reforms. (Compare 2 Chronicles 34:1-7.)

- How active a role do you think Josiah played as king before he was an adult?
- If Josiah wasn't really ruling the nation during the early years of his reign, who was? Why doesn't Scripture say more about the ones who actually ruled for the boy king?
- What, do you think, was Josiah taught about how he should act as king?
- In what ways are the policies of our nation's government influenced by people who spend their lives serving different leaders? Who are some of the people "behind the scenes" who have influence over the president or prime minister, for example?

Both 2 Kings and 2 Chronicles date the discovery of the Book of the Law to the eighteenth year of Josiah's reign. Scholars believe that this Book of the Law was probably a version of what we now know as Deuteronomy.

- Where do you suppose this book was found?
- Assume for it moment that the whereabouts of the Book of the Law had been known in Manasseh's day. Why wouldn't it have been brought forward then?
- When the Law is read (2 Kings 22:11), Josiah seems shocked to learn of the many ways the people have disobeyed God. How, do you think, could the nation have strayed so far from God without realizing it?
- Are there ways that you think people in our own society (including Christians) have unwittingly strayed from God? Explain.

Convicted

Read Deuteronomy 28:15-68. When Josiah hears these words, he becomes aware just how far the people have strayed from the God's Law.

- According to the Deuteronomy text, what would happen to the people if they disobeyed the Law of God? Why was Josiah worried?
- Using the list about Manasseh's sins that you made earlier (page 59), skim though Deuteronomy and look for things that occurred during his reign that violated the Law.

The prophet Huldah (a woman) has good news and bad news for Josiah. (See 2 Kings 22:14-20.)

- Why isn't Josiah to receive the full brunt of God's wrath? Why won't God relent from punishment? Why would the Lord punish the people for the leadership of Manasseh?
- Josiah takes steps to bring the people back under the Law. What are they?

What exactly does Josiah's command mean to "keep the passover to the LORD"? The text says that no such passover had been kept since the days of the judges, more than four centuries earlier. Had passover, which recalled God's delivery of the Israelites from slavery in Egypt, been forgotten? Not exactly. But passover had become a family celebration held in individual homes. The passover to the Lord ordered by Josiah was to be a national, public celebration, as outlined in the Book of Deuteronomy, which the workmen had discovered in the Temple.

62

The End

Josiah is the last king of Judah who was not a puppet of a foreign power. Near the end of Josiah's reign, Babylon (which ultimately would destroy Judah) fought against Egypt. The Egyptian Pharaoh Neco attempted to bring his army through Judah to reach Babylonian territory. Although the Egyptians had no quarrel with Judah, Josiah attempted to block them. He died in battle from wounds suffered at Megiddo in 609 B.C.

As the prophet Huldah foretold, Josiah did not live to see the people carried into exile in Babylon. His son Jehoahaz succeeded him; three months later, Jehoahaz was removed by Pharaoh and replaced by a puppet king from Egypt. Eleven years after that, the Babylonians, who had defeated Egypt, installed their own puppet king.

- The Bible gives no reason why Josiah chose to fight Pharaoh, instead of letting his army pass through Judah. Why, do you think, might he have fought?
- Read 2 Chronicles 35:20-24 for an alternative account of these events. How does this text add to your understanding of Josiah's actions?

After Looking at Both the Text and the Context . . .

- What new insights do you have?

- What stands out in the story?

- What answers did you find to questions you raised earlier?

- What new questions do you have?

- If rulers or leaders are not faithful to God's covenant, are the people "off the hook"? What role or responsibility do they have?

- If government leaders today are making decisions that you understand to be not in keeping with God's Law and desires for the people, what can you do?

- What one learning will you take from this Scripture and apply to your life?

Choose one or more of Views A, B, and C to discuss; **OR** have different small groups talk about one and then summarize the discussion for the other groups. **Be sure to have everyone complete View U.**

Conviction of the Spirit

Josiah undergoes a transformation when he realizes that the nation he leads (and, presumably, himself) had disobeyed God's Law. A simple definition of *sin* is "being separated from God." Scripture describes people suddenly experiencing their sin as a sense of separation from God. (See Isaiah 6:5 and Luke 5:8.)

- Have you ever experienced a profound sense that you had separated yourself from God by the things you have done?
- What sorts of things separate us from God?

Christians sometimes see the laws of Deuteronomy and Leviticus as having little to do with our lives. As a group, study Deuteronomy 8.

- How do these Scriptures apply to your life?
- How do they apply to the life of your nation?

Repent literally means to "turn around." As used in Scripture, it means to turn your life back toward God.

- In what ways do Josiah and the people of Judah repent?
- How do you measure true repentance?
- How do we turn our lives toward God?
- In what areas do you need to repent?
- How does a nation turn its life toward God?

How Do We Lose the Law of God?

Workmen find the Book of the Law in the Temple.

- Where do you think the book had been?
- If the book had been found before Josiah's reign, why wouldn't it have been brought out earlier?

When Josiah hears the Law, he realizes that he and his people have been living in disobedience to God. Not only were altars to other gods spread throughout the land, but such altars and idols were in the Temple itself. To comply with the Law, the people would have to make major changes in the way they lived.

- How does a society lose the Law of God? Is it possible to lose sight of God's Law without fully realizing it? Explain.
- In your opinion, has your nation lost the Law of God? If so, in what ways?
- Is it possible for a nation to enforce God's Law? Why, or why not?

Led to God or Away From God?

The story of Josiah suggests that our leaders can lead us toward or away from God. Manasseh and other kings led Judah away from God. Josiah was credited with leading Judah back toward God.

- Do you think that a leader today can lead a nation toward or away from God? Can you give some contemporary examples?
- Are we at the mercy of our leaders' religious convictions? Do you think that God punishes nations whose leaders are unfaithful and rewards those whose leaders remain faithful? Explain.
- In what sense was Israel a "nation" even in exile? Does God determine what constitutes a nation the same way that humans determine what constitutes a nation?
- In what sense is the church universal, the body of Christ, a nation? Can the church be led astray by its leaders?

Many people in Jerusalem (the prophet Jeremiah, for one) probably felt as Josiah did upon hearing the Book of the Law. Yet only Josiah was guaranteed that he would live out his life in peace.

- How do you react to the idea that you might be punished as part of an "unfaithful nation"?

 **Closer, Lord, Closer**

As you listen to and read the news this week, consider the events described in relation to your understanding of God's Law.

• In what ways is your nation living according to the Law of God?

• In what ways is your nation moving away from God?

Conviction is a gift of the Spirit. During your prayer time this week, pray to God for conviction. Pray that God will show you how you are moving away from God in your life and how you can grow closer to God.

Check *www.ileadyouth.com/3V* for worship suggestions.

Miss Courageous

Esther 4:12-17

When you hear the term *beauty queen,* does the word *courageous* come to mind? Probably not. We tend to associate Miss America or Miss Universe with one attribute only: physical beauty. Esther, too, became a queen because of her looks. Fortunately for her people, she had a lot more going for her than that.

¹² When they told Mordecai what Esther had said, ¹³ Mordecai told them to reply to Esther, "Do not think that in the king's palace you will escape any more than all the other Jews. ¹⁴ For if you keep silence at such a time as this, relief and deliverance will rise for the Jews from another quarter, but you and your father's family will perish. Who knows? Perhaps you have come to royal dignity for just such a time as this." ¹⁵ Then Esther said in reply to Mordecai, ¹⁶ "Go, gather all the Jews to be found in Susa, and hold a fast on my behalf, and neither eat nor drink for three days, night or day. I and my maids will also fast as you do. After that I will go to the king, though it is against the law; and if I perish, I perish." ¹⁷ Mordecai then went away and did everything as Esther had ordered him.

Esther 4:12-17

Read the passage aloud. Have others read silently from different translations and report any differences in the wording.

• How do the differences help you understand the text?

• What questions do the differences raise for you?

Highlight words or phrases in the text that you think are important. List any questions the text raises for you.

• What do you think Mordecai's first statement in verse 14 means? How is that a statement of faith?

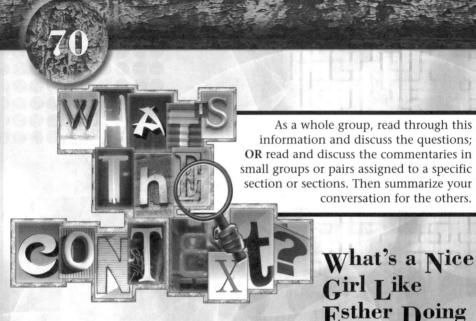

As a whole group, read through this information and discuss the questions; OR read and discuss the commentaries in small groups or pairs assigned to a specific section or sections. Then summarize your conversation for the others.

What's a Nice Girl Like Esther Doing in a Place Like This?

The story of Esther is set in the royal court of Persia (modern Iran). Decades earlier, the Jewish people had been conquered and taken into exile by the Babylonians. When the Persians conquered Babylon, the Jews became subjects of the Persian king Xerxes (whose name appears in the Bible story in its Greek rendering, Ahasuerus).

Under Persian rule, the Jews were allowed to begin returning to Jerusalem. Before that happened, however, Esther and her uncle Mordecai—who raised the young girl after her parents died—became part of the Persian king's court.

Mordecai seems to have been a minor official, chosen for his administrative ability. Esther was chosen for her great beauty to join the king's harem—a stable of young women who served as concubines or secondary wives. Just as Joseph rose to a high position in Egypt, and Daniel and his friends rose to prominence during the Exile in Babylon, Esther and Mordecai prospered too. Mordecai gained favor by getting word to the king of an assassination plot by his servants. Esther, meanwhile, became so much the king's favorite that he named her as his queen and told her that he would give her anything she asked for—even as much as half of his kingdom.

- Have you known anyone who received preferential treatment because of his or her appearance (or for other reasons that had nothing to do with ability or accomplishment)? How did you feel about it?
- Did you ever receive such special treatment (such as being a teacher's pet)? How did others react?
- If you were in a privileged position, how would it be difficult to look out for the interests of others who were being treated unfairly?

Esther's Holiday

Haman was a high official in the Persian government, second only to the king. Haman hated Esther's uncle Mordecai. Because Mordecai worshiped God, he would not bow down to Haman, which made Haman furious. In his anger, Haman hatched a plot to dupe the king into agreeing to the extermination of all Jews in the kingdom. (Read Esther 3:5-12.)

When Mordecai learned of the plot, he went to Esther and urged her to see the king and plead for the lives of her fellow Jews. Now read Esther 7 to learn how Esther exposed Haman's treachery. She not only saves the people, but Mordecai winds up as the king's second in command!

Esther's story is the basis for the Jewish holiday Purim. It is a time for a real celebration when members of the Jewish community gather to read the Book of Esther (once during the day and once at night) and celebrate how they were saved from Haman's plot.

Purim is observed on the 14th day of the Jewish month of Adar, the day after all of the Jews were to be killed. This usually falls in March, but since the Jewish calendar is lunar (based on the moon), the actual date of Purim each year moves around on the calendar that most of us use.

- What hidden qualities does Esther reveal in bringing Haman's plot to light?
- Who do you think played the greater role here: Esther or Mordecai?
- What qualities does King Ahasuerus display?
- The prophet Isaiah describes Cyrus, the Persian ruler who allowed the Jews to return home, as God's chosen one (Isaiah 44:28–45:13). What might this suggest about God's role in Esther's story?

The Book That Almost Wasn't

The books of the Bible didn't just collect themselves. A number of books were circulating that could have been included. Someone had to decide which books would be included and which would not.

In the case of the Tanach, or Hebrew Bible (what Christians call the Old Testament), the final decision hadn't been made even in the time of Jesus. Of course, the Torah (the first five books of the Bible) was in. So were the prophets. Then there were the "Writings." Not everyone agreed on which of these should be included. Some said that the book named for Esther (whose Hebrew name is Hadassah) should not be included because it never specifically mentions God.

Others argued that God is woven through the entire story. God's concern for the people and God's call to Esther through Mordecai are important themes. In fact, portions of the Jewish tradition regard God's name as so holy that it is never mentioned. If people want to refer to God, they simply say "HaShem," which means "the Name." So just because God's name isn't mentioned, doesn't mean that the writer and storyteller didn't think that God was involved in the story. Those who saw God in the story carried the day, and Esther became a book of the Jewish and Christian Bibles.

- Does the fact that humans chose which books would be included in the Bible affect your view of the Bible's authority in your life? How? Why?
- List some of the ways you see God at work in this story. Why, do you think, doesn't the text mention God specifically?
- In what ways that are not formally noticed do you see God at work in your community? in your school? in your church?

After Looking at Both the Text and the Context . . .

Deal with some or all of these questions before moving to What's Next?

- What new insights do you have?

- Which characters or events stand out for you? Why?

- What answers did you find to the questions raised earlier?

List any new questions that you have.

- What do you think makes a book a good candidate for being part of the Bible?

- If you were to choose a biblical character on whom to base a holiday, who would it be?

- What would have happened had Esther not acted? What do you think motivated her to act?

- When have you been put in a situation where it was up to you to make a difference? What difference did you make?

- What one learning will you take from this text and apply to your life?

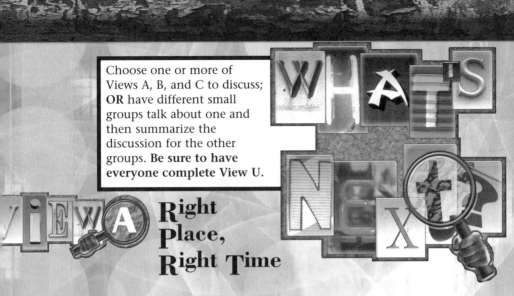

Choose one or more of Views A, B, and C to discuss; **OR** have different small groups talk about one and then summarize the discussion for the other groups. **Be sure to have everyone complete View U.**

VIEW A Right Place, Right Time

When Mordecai discovers Haman's plot to kill all of the Jews, he wants Esther to talk the king into saving the lives of the Jews. But there's a problem with this plan: Queen Esther had not ever let the king know that she was Jewish.

Esther has to wonder, *Will this bit of information change the way that the king feels about me?* If she tells the king about her background only now, will he feel that she had lied to him and is untrustworthy? Will the hot-tempered king be angry? Will he order that she be killed along with the other Jews? Esther doesn't know.

But she must answer for herself the biggest question: Will she risk her neck for her people?

Mordecai tells Esther, "Perhaps you were born for just such a time as this." Is she the right person in the right place at the right time to do the right thing? Are you?

- Have you ever chosen not to tell someone something about yourself because you were afraid of what he or she might think? Explain.
- Have you ever been in a situation in which you felt that you were the right person in the right place at the right time to do the right thing? How did you respond? How did you know what was the right thing to do?
- Where do you see God in such situations?

75

  **Pretty Is as Pretty Does**

Maybe you've heard the old saying "Pretty is as pretty does." If you haven't, it's a good saying to remember. It means that the way people act is more important than how they look. We probably all know someone who looks great but acts snobby and superior to everybody else. On the other hand, we also know people who might not be considered beautiful or handsome but who treat others in such a welcoming way they that they take on a different kind of beauty, a beauty that comes from the inside.

There's another old saying: "You can't judge a book by its cover." In other words, the way people look does not tell you what they are really like inside. Actually, looks tell us very little about a person. Some people who had been able to see and then lost their sight confess how much they used to judge others on their appearance and how silly they now feel that was.

At the beginning of this story (Esther 1), King Ahasuerus demands that his queen Vashti come to a party that he was throwing for his friends and parade her beauty. When she refuses, the King gets rid of her and sets about selecting a new queen from his harem. That's where Esther comes in. After a year in the king's harem, Esther has received a lot of beauty treatments. But she turns out to be much more than just a pretty face.

- Why, do you think, may Queen Vashti have refused to obey the king's command? What lessons do you think Esther drew from Vashti's experience? How do you think the incident with Vashti affected Esther's decision to come to the king's court without an invitation?
- Have you ever judged anyone based on his or her looks? What kind of judgment did you make? After you got to know the person, how accurate was your initial impression?
- How do you come to know what a person is really like?

 **M**iss **C**ourageous

In beauty pageants, certain participants receive special recognition. The movie *Miss Congeniality* gets its title from one of those special awards. The title Miss Congeniality is given to the contestant who reaches out in friendship to the other participants. Maybe Sandra Bullock's character in the film should have been called Miss Courageous. She is an unlikely contestant anyway, since she is really working undercover to save the lives of the other contestants.

Esther needed courage for two reasons. First, if she revealed that she was a Jew, she could have been killed. Second, a law of the king's court stated that if anyone entered the king's presence without being invited by the king, he or she could be killed. This law applied even to the queen.

Esther prepares to see the king by fasting and praying, rather than by doing exercises and receiving beauty treatments. She asks Mordecai to fast and pray too. She tells him that she will go see the king, and "If I die, I die." Perhaps Esther should have the title Miss Courageous.

- Have you ever been asked to do something that was really scary for you, even though it would benefit someone else? Explain.
- How did you respond?
- Describe a time when you (or someone else) stood up for someone even though it put you (or that someone else) at risk.
- Whom do you know that you would give the title Miss or Mr. Courageous? Why?
- What do fasting and praying have to do with courage? Explain.

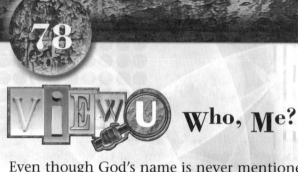 **Who, Me?**

Even though God's name is never mentioned, it's pretty clear that Esther has a very important calling from God. It's easy to look for God in a worship service or to talk about God in Sunday school. The Book of Esther tells about God, who is also in the very decisions we make every day.

What if you are just the right person at the right place at the right time for some decision that will touch the lives of others? Your choices may not be as dramatic as Esther's, but even a kind or encouraging word might make a huge difference to a friend who is depressed.

Perhaps one of our callings from God is to look for those times when our choices can make a real difference.

- How can you tell when a decision might make a big difference to someone else?
- Is it possible to live as if every decision might just be that "big decision"? Explain.

This week think about these lines, attributed to St. Teresa of Avila: "Christ has no hands but my hands, no feet but my feet."

- Where have you been placed in a position to be Christ's hands on earth?

Check *www.ileadyouth.com/3V*
for worship suggestions.

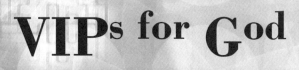

VIPs for God

Daniel 1:8-12

Have you ever been a teacher's pet when you didn't really want to be? Or received special treatment in ways that made you feel uncomfortable? Welcome to Daniel's world. Sometimes, getting the V.I.P. treatment can tempt you to compromise your guiding principles. But as Daniel found, staying faithful to God—and remembering whose child you are—offers rewards of its own.

8 But Daniel resolved that he would not defile himself with the royal rations of food and wine; so he asked the palace master to allow him not to defile himself. 9 Now God allowed Daniel to receive favor and compassion from the palace master. 10 The palace master said to Daniel, "I am afraid of my lord the king; he has appointed your food and your drink. If he should see you in poorer condition than the other young men of your own age, you would endanger my head with the king." 11 Then Daniel asked the guard whom the palace master had appointed over Daniel, Hananiah, Mishael, and Azariah: 12 "Please test your servants for ten days. Let us be given vegetables to eat and water to drink."

Daniel 1:8-12

Read the passage aloud. Have others read silently from different translations and report any differences in the wording.

• How do the differences help you understand the text?

• What questions do the differences raise for you?

Highlight words or phrases in the text that you feel are important. List any questions the text raises for you.

Invite participants to present a skit in which they ask an authority figure to bend the rules to accommodate a special need. How about a classroom setting? a sports activity? with parents?

• What new insights did the skit give to the Scripture? Add these to the list.

• What new information does this dramatization reveal about the boldness of Daniel and his friends? Add these highlights to your list.

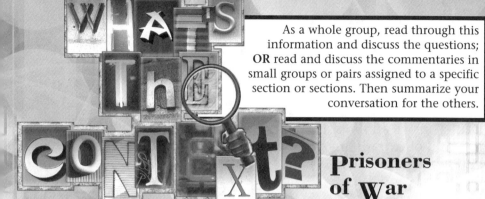

As a whole group, read through this information and discuss the questions; OR read and discuss the commentaries in small groups or pairs assigned to a specific section or sections. Then summarize your conversation for the others.

Prisoners of War

Throughout their history, the Israelites had a difficult time obeying God. God regularly gave them chances to repent, but the Israelites continued to worship other gods. To punish them or redirect their behavior, God sometimes allowed the Israelites' enemies to defeat them. They had a long list of foes. In Daniel 1:1-2, God allowed the Babylonian Empire (modern-day Iraq), under King Nebuchadnezzar, to conquer the Israelites; destroy Jerusalem and the Temple; and take the people into exile, where they remained for 50 years. In short, they were prisoners of war.

The Babylonians worshiped their own gods and not the God of Israel. In exile, the Israelites were away from their place of worship and were immersed into a culture that was contrary to their religious way of life. You can imagine how the Babylonian experience put pressure on the Israelites to maintain their faithfulness to God.

- What does the history of the Israelites say about God's relationship with human beings?
- What does it reveal about God's character?
- Why, do you think, did King Nebuchadnezzar bring the Israelites to Babylon as prisoners of war? List reasons.
- How do you think the people felt as prisoners of war? Read Psalm 137 for some hints.
- How would it be tempting, under the circumstances, for Israelites like Daniel to begin worshiping the gods of the Babylonians?

81

Roll Call

In exile, Daniel and his fellow Jews were subjects of the Babylonian empire. And naturally, King Nebuchadnezzar wanted to put his brightest and most talented subjects to work for him in building that empire.

Daniel and his friends, Hananiah, Mishael, and Azariah, were just the kind of extraordinary people the king wanted. Daniel had the gift of prophecy. He interpreted the dreams of King Nebuchadnezzar (chapters 2 and 4) and the vision of the handwriting on the wall for King Belshazzar (chapter 5). Daniel's prophetic gifts enabled him to enjoy high status in Babylon.

Because they were VIPs, the four received Babylonian names: Belshazzar (Daniel); Shadrach (Hananiah); Meshach (Mishael); and Abednego (Azariah). They also were to receive the choicest foods.

But these men are VIPs in God's eyes for a very different reason: their unshakable faith. In the study text, refusing to eat the food of the Babylonians is an act of faithfulness to God. So is the refusal of Shadrach, Meshach, and Abednego to obey King Nebuchadnezzar's law to worship a golden statue (read Daniel 3:8-28)—even though it lands them in a fiery furnace. Years later, after the Persians have conquered Babylon, Daniel remains faithful to God by refusing a decree that requires all subjects to pray to King Darius. (Read Daniel 6:6-28.)

Read Daniel 1:3-7.

- List the qualities the king saw as extraordinary. Do you disagree or agree with the king's definition? Why?
- Societies often define extraordinary people based upon physical characteristics. Why?
- In your experience, how does God define extraordinary people?
- For Daniel and his friends, what were the positive consequences of being chosen as extraordinary? the negative consequences?
- Review the stories of the fiery furnace (Daniel 3:8-30) and Daniel in the lions' den (Daniel 6:1-26a). How does the faithfulness of the four friends lead others to recognize and praise God?

Daniel's Diet

As faithful Jews, Daniel and his friends regarded certain foods as unclean. They stuck to foods allowed by God under the Law of Moses (see Leviticus 11:1-45). Scavenger animals and pigs were unclean. Eating an unclean animal was unthinkable.

The major portion of an Israelite's diet consisted of bread and vegetables. Meat was a special treat because the animals were needed for their wool, milk, or labor.

The Babylonians had no such customs. They ate and drank anything. In this story, King Nebuchadnezzar wants Daniel and his friends to eat the same meat as the king eats. The text does not reveal what type of meat this might have been, only that it was unclean food that would "defile" these Jews. For Daniel and his friends, eating the royal rations would be a sin against God.

- What does the text suggest about the reasons the king wanted the chosen young men to eat the royal rations?
- How would diet relate to the goal of immersing Daniel and his friends into the Babylonian culture?
- How does the saying "You are what you eat" relate to this story?
- Look up *defile* in a dictionary. How does this word add to your understanding of Daniel's insistence on eating vegetables and water?

Free Trial Offer

At first, Daniel's request to the palace master (Daniel 1:8-11) seems applicable only to Daniel. But he knows that his friends are also at risk of defilement. Fearful that a diet without fat will make them weaklings—and that he will be executed if he fails in his responsibility to keep them strong and healthy—the palace master seeks more information from Daniel. He sincerely wants to help.

Daniel thinks of a way to address the guard's fears. He tells the guard to give them only vegetables and water for ten days; and if they are not presentable for the king, then they will eat the royal diet. In this way, Daniel turns a potential enemy into a trusted friend.

- How did the ten-day time period build a trusted relationship between the palace master and Daniel?
- What does this conversation between Daniel and the palace master reveal about Daniel's character? about his relationship with God? Make a list of his character traits.
- Why, do you think, does the palace master grant Daniel's request? What did he have to lose?
- Using this story, what are some of the character traits you would ascribe to the palace master? What does the story suggest about the relationship between God and people outside our faith?
- How does this story reveal Daniel to be an extraordinary person?

After Looking at Both the Text and the Context . . .

Deal with some or all of these questions
before moving to What's Next?

- What new insights do you have?

- What does this text say about faith?

- In what ways do you identify with Daniel and his friends? with the palace master?

- How does God show favor to us?

- What extraordinary characteristics do you admire in others?

- What are some extraordinary characteristics you see in yourself? List them.

- How important is our diet in our relationship with God? How can what we choose to eat possibly relate to honoring God?

- What one learning will you take from this Scripture and apply to your life?

Choose one or more of Views A, B, and C to discuss; **OR** have different small groups talk about one and then summarize the discussion for the other groups. **Be sure to have everyone complete View U.**

 **Favorites**

At some time or another, all of us have been in situations where someone played favorites and we weren't the favored ones. As Daniel's story showed, being the favorite can bring us problems too.

The Jews in Babylon believed that God had rejected them; they were no longer God's favored people. Then when Daniel and his friends were chosen for special treatment by the king, Babylonians resented them and set them up in situations where they had to choose between worshiping God and bowing before idols.

Daniel's story teaches us that we are always God's "favorite." There may be times when we think that God has turned against us and is blessing everyone else. We may feel as if we're in captivity. Daniel reminds us that if we keep the faith, we can experience the favor of God in any situation.

• Work in groups to discuss times when you have experienced favor from other people, such as teachers, parents, teachers, friends, or coaches. Then discuss times when you were not the favorite. How did you feel? How did you respond? What impact have those experiences had on you?

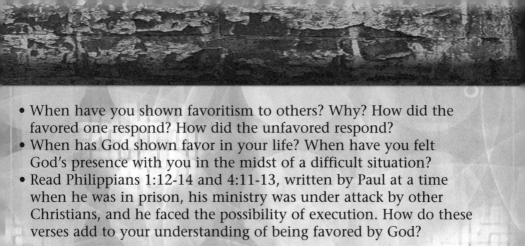

- When have you shown favoritism to others? Why? How did the favored one respond? How did the unfavored respond?
- When has God shown favor in your life? When have you felt God's presence with you in the midst of a difficult situation?
- Read Philippians 1:12-14 and 4:11-13, written by Paul at a time when he was in prison, his ministry was under attack by other Christians, and he faced the possibility of execution. How do these verses add to your understanding of being favored by God?

The VIP Treatment

Being a VIP in our society is often based on an abundance of money, fame, or power. Not many of us have those. Yet think about the truly extraordinary people you have known: teachers, community volunteers, coaches, custodians, your parents. Most don't have what it takes to be on the A list in our culture. They may do jobs that often get little recognition.

But all of us are very important persons in God's eyes. God's grace has nothing to do with how much we own; it has everything to do with those gifts we have. King Nebuchadnezzar made Daniel and his friends VIPs because of their abilities. In God's eyes, however, they became extraordinary Old Testament people because of their extraordinary faith.

- Make a list of some of the people you know who make vital contributions but are often unrecognized or underappreciated? Why did you choose each of the people on your list? What makes each a VIP in your eyes?
- Look again at the list you created (page 82) of traits that seemed important to King Nebuchadnezzar when he chose Daniel and his friends to become royal pages in his court (Daniel 1:3-5). Evaluate the class, gender, and racial implications. Do we use these same kinds of measurements?
- Think about entertainment and sports celebrities. Do we look more favorably on famous people than we view others who are less wealthy or less well known? Why?
- Review the list you made earlier (page 84) of Daniel's character traits. Did you include humility? How did you define it? Read Matthew 23:10-12. What is the relationship between humility and greatness?

# VIEW C Soul Food

In a real way, we are what we eat. Research reveals that how we eat has a huge impact not just on our bodies, but on our emotions and energy levels. Our eating habits are directly connected to our feelings about ourselves, our environment, and God. Our spiritual health and strength have a lot to do with how we treat our bodies.

The palace master was concerned about the physical well-being of Daniel and his friends. Daniel was concerned about how eating Babylonian foods would affect their spiritual well-being.

In the early church, one of the biggest conflicts between Jewish Christians and Gentile Christians related to diet. Some Jewish Christians were convinced that all believers must maintain a Jewish diet. However, Peter and Paul explained that salvation depended not on diet, but on faith in Jesus Christ.

- What is the importance of food in your culture, community, family, and church?
- In what ways (if any) do you believe that food is essential to the soul?
- Why, do you think, did many early Jewish Christians want to retain their former religious traditions related to diet?

Read Acts 11:4-10.

- What does Peter's dream mean to you?
- How is the welcoming of different foods a reflection of God's love for all people, both Jews and Gentiles?
- Take a few minutes to write down what you ate today and yesterday. Beside each item, record how you felt when you ate it.
- How do the media and our culture contribute the use of food in harmful ways, such as eating disorders, obesity, and dangerous crash diets? Why do we call some items "junk food"?

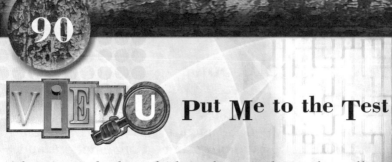

Put Me to the Test

Advertisers who have faith in their products often offer a free trial or a money-back guarantee. Daniel suggested a trial period to the palace master because he also had faith and was sure that God would help him meet the challenge.

As you face your challenges in life, people will question your abilities, strength, and faith. Instead of giving in to these doubts, consider how God made Daniel and his friends VIPs in response to their faithfulness during a time of trial.

In this space, or on a separate sheet of paper, write your reflections about these questions:

• What challenges is God calling me to meet?

• Am I willing to be put to the test?

Check **www.ileadyouth.com/3V**
for worship suggestions.